Mysterious Milton Keynes

James Willis

*'There are more things in heaven and earth, Horatio,
Than are dreamt of in your philosophy'*

William Shakespeare. Hamlet, Act 1, Scene 5.

This edition published in Great Britain in 2013 by DB Publishing, an imprint of JMD Media.

Copyright © James Willis, 2013

ISBN 9781780912035

Mysterious
Milton Keynes

CONTENTS

INTRODUCTION

Milton Keynes – more than meets the eye

To the uninitiated, the very mention of Milton Keynes conjures up images of roundabouts, concrete cows, centralized planning and 1960's urban architecture; a vast, bland network of housing estates, a city with no history, and one which - in the popular imagination – cannot hope to compete with the likes of Edinburgh, London, Oxford or any of the other historical British stalwarts when it comes to mystery and intrigue.

But scratch below the surface, and one will discover not only a secret past but also a secret present: a living, breathing and very quirky history in the making. Milton Keynes, together with its satellite settlements, constitutes a composite patchwork of the ancient and modern, the urban and the rural, all stitched together with enough corresponding myth, paranormal activity, conspiracy, folklore, superstition and urban legend to give many a more established haunt a good run for it's money.

Behind the façade of our structured and well-ordered reality, there lurks a shadowy, alternate truth which does not sit comfortably with our accepted understanding in an age of reason. Wonders abound, which – though they may not easily be explained – nevertheless bring colour, enchantment and magic into an otherwise predictable world.

Once you've read this book, you will never look at the grid roads, manicured lawns and bygone churches of Milton Keynes in the same light again.

Welcome to the mysterious world of Milton Keynes....

PART I

Earth Mysteries, Geography and Features

Milton Keynes – formally established as a unitary urban entity on the 23rd January 1967 -   was conceived, designed, and always intended to be - a city: the local authority, official literature, maps and residents refer to it as such, and it is the term which will be used throughout this book. Yet the reality is that Milton Keynes, despite it's lofty aspirations and a quarter of million residents, remains technically a town, it's latest application for city status having been rejected in 2012.

Whilst much of the thirty four square mile city was built on farmland, a significant number of small towns, villages and other settlements were swallowed up within the artificial borders. All of this land has a long, rich and well documented history dating back to at least the Bronze Age.

Less well documented, however, are the many strange geographical features of the *modern* Milton Keynes. One day these curious features may leave future archaeologists scratching their heads and looking for meaning.

Ley Lines

In 1921, British brewer Alfred Watkins observed that many significant landmarks such as churches, ancient mounds, peaks, stone circles and sacred sites appeared to be linked by a network of pathways and tracks. To his astonishment he found that these pathways frequently formed straight lines across the country. Researching this concept further, Watkins concluded that numerous long lost pathways could easily be rediscovered by studying maps and connecting up known paths with eminent ancient sites. Watkins believed that these straight lines marked out long lost trade routes, and he coined the term 'ley lines' to describe them. The theory of ley lines thus began to take hold, and over the next few decades various new age philosophers began to ascribe many other attributes to them, ranging from the possession of feng-shui type energy to magnetism, healing powers and spiritual significance.

Milton Keynes is said to sit upon a ley line, and many of the city's most prominent major (as well as many minor) features are aligned upon it. The 'Midsummer ley line,' as it is known, cuts a straight line through:-

- The island in Willen Lake North (see Part 6: Disappearing Goats).
- The Medicine Wheel stone circle (see Part 1: Standing Stones and Neolithic Monuments).
- The city's famous Tree Cathedral in Newlands (the ley line runs directly up the nave).
- The Belvedere (highest point in Milton Keynes).
- Directly down Midsummer Boulevard (the main road at the heart of the city).
- The train station.

The ley line continues in a straight line all the way to the mystical Glastonbury Tor (see Part 4: Glastonbury Thorn) in Somerset.

'The Gnomon' is an ominous looking structure which can be found on the Midsummer ley line between the Tree Cathedral and the Belvedere, immediately adjacent to the cricket pavilion in Campbell Park. Whilst many believe that The Gnomon, which was created by Peter Bowker in 1994, is simply a representation of three cricket stumps and a ball (which is understandable given that it overlooks the cricket pitch), there is a far deeper meaning hidden behind it. The word *gnomon* is derived from the ancient Greek word meaning 'indicator' or 'that which reveals', and the term is now applied to the vertical pin which casts a shadow on a sundial. The Milton Keynes Gnomon (or *Shadow Caster*) is designed to cast it's shadow directly along the Midsummer ley line. In addition to it's special positioning and properties, the enormous, untreated slate stones from which The Gnomon is constructed evoke an obvious comparison with more ancient megalithic structures (see Part 1: Standing Stones and Neolithic Monuments).

Midsummer Sunrise

Unbeknown to thousands of commuters and residents, Milton Keynes was - in part - inspired by, and planned upon, principles more famously encapsulated in a most ancient and mystical monument: Stonehenge.

At the heart of Milton Keynes lies it's main road - *Midsummer Boulevard.* The Midsummer ley line runs directly down the centre of Midsum-

The Gnomon

mer Boulevard (see Part 1: Ley Lines). It is from this 'spine' that the famous grid roads emanate, and from which the town takes its shape. Midsummer Boulevard - like Stonehenge - was designed so that it aligns directly with the sunrise on the summer solstice (roughly 45 degrees from north), hence its name.

At the bottom of Midsummer Boulevard, sitting at the south-western end of central Milton Keynes, is the train station. The train station is a huge, glass fronted building resembling a gigantic mirror. On the 21st June (summer solstice) the sun rises directly over the Belvedere (a hill in Campbell Park which is the highest point in the city). The sun's rays then shine down the ley line of Midsummer Boulevard and hit the mirrored train station directly: given the right atmospheric conditions this can be a most spectacular sight.

Milton Keynes – an entire city aligned on the midsummer sunrise.

The Belvedere

Standing Stones and Neolithic Monuments

Much of the British and European landscape is dotted with Neolithic monuments, mounds and standing stones: speculation as to their original purpose abounds, with theories covering everything from human sacrifice to astrology. The mystery of these the ancient structures is perpetuated and honoured in a contemporary fashion throughout present day Milton Keynes, in what might be termed 'neo-Neolithic' monuments.

The most obvious homage can be found in the Theatre District of the city centre. In what Milton Keynes Council describe as a 'family garden' stands a scaled down replica of Stonehenge. The structure was designed by Pauley Landscapes to *'represent civilization, mankind and the universe'*.

The Milton Keynes Stonehenge

A significantly larger stone circle can be found on the shores of Willen Lake, in Willen North Park. Sitting directly on the Midsummer ley line - from which it is said to draw power - one can find the *Medicine Wheel*.

The Medicine Wheel was ostensibly built to celebrate the Millennium. Much has been much written about the Wheel, it's purpose and it's design. The facts can best be summed up as follows:-

The Medicine Wheel

- The Medicine Wheel is made up of one hundred and eight limestone rocks from the village of Weston Underwood.
- The Wheel draws inspiration from Native North American Medicine Wheels as well as the stone circles which can be found all over the British Isles.
- The Wheel consists of two concentric circles.
- The outer and inner circles are said to symbolise our outer and inner worlds, the universe and humanity within.
- The Wheel has four large gateways which represent the four compass points, the seasons, the main human races and the four elements.
- The two lesser gateways on the outer circle are aligned along the Milton Keynes midsummer ley line.
- There is a single flat stone lying to the south east of the East Gate, known as The Africa Stone - this provides a link to the Kalahari Bush people who have built their own 'Circle of Hearts Medicine Wheel' in the Kalahari desert.
- In the centre of the Medicine Wheel is the 'Sacred Fire' which is lit during ceremonies. The ash is retained at the nearby Buddhist temple. This Sacred Fire represents 'the Sacred Spirit in all things, places, people, and for all time.'
- Some people believe that prayers offered at the centre of the

Wheel are somehow 'amplified.'
- The Wheel was designed by Roy Littlesun, the adopted son of a Native American elder named Titus Quomayumptewa.
- Native American Chiefs from the Onodage tribe travelled to Milton Keynes and consecrated the completed Wheel with prayer and the smoking of peace pipes.
- The Wheel is looked after by the Guardians of The Wheel, who are drawn from the volunteers who co-ordinated and assisted in its construction.
- The Medicine Wheel attracts many pagans at certain times of the year (see Part 4: Witches, Pagans and Satanists).

Three further stone circles, made up of around one hundred separate limestone boulders, can be found alongside the Grand Union Canal in Great Linford, between St Andrews Church and Church Lees.

The biggest standing stones of all can be seen on a hill overlooking the Milton Keynes Coachway (coach station), just off Junction 14 of the M1.

As well as building complex stone circles, the ancient British tribes also had a propensity towards more simple, isolated stones known as *menhirs*. Most of Britain's lonely menhirs have stood upon remote Scottish islands or isolated Cornish moors for thousands of years. As with most Neolithic structures, the purpose of the original menhirs is open to question: the most popular theories hold that the stones were used as waymarkers, boundary markers, astrological tools, to mark burial sites, or for spiritual or social rituals.

There are several menhirs dotted around Milton Keynes, albeit they are considerably younger than the mighty monoliths upon which they are based. One of the biggest – a single stone standing at least eleven foot high - can be found on the footpath by White Horse Drive in Emerson Valley. Other large stones can be found on the riverside footpath which runs between the Old Stratford Bridge and Wolverton, and on the roadside adjacent to the Galley Hill roundabout, south east of Stony Stratford.

Two of the Great Linford Circles.

The giant stones overlooking The Coachway'

Eleven foot high menhir on White Horse Drive, Emerson Valley

Neolithic inspiration can be seen in the names of the city streets as well as it's architecture. *Avebury Boulevard* is the adjacent, southern parallel to Midsummer Boulevard (see Part 1: Midsummer sunrise). Avebury Boulevard is named after the largest stone circle in the world which can be found in the village of Avebury, a few miles to the north of Stonehenge. The adjacent northern parallel to Midsummer Boulevard is known as *Silbury Boulevard*. Silbury Boulevard is named after a Neolithic chalk mound in Wiltshire which is believed to be the largest man made pre-historic structure in Europe.

The very fabric of Milton Keynes is now a living homage to the mystery and esotericism of the ancients. Five thousand years from now, perhaps the purpose and meaning of the 'Milton Keynes Monuments' will be subject to a similar debate to that which surrounds the originals today.

The Great Pyramids of Milton Keynes

The symbolism of the pyramid is legendary. To the ancient Egyptians the pyramids represented a path to the afterlife, and they famously built the most magnificent structures in which to entomb and honour their dead. To the Aztecs, pyramids were conduits to otherworldly power, and humans were sacrificed atop the summits. To the Mesopotamians, their gigantic ziggurats (terraced, stepped pyramids) represented holy mountains and acted as shrines to local gods. Biblical scholars believe that the tower of Babel - described in the Old Testament as man's attempt to reach heaven - was itself a huge ziggurat. It is clear that to many ancient and powerful cultures, the pyramid and it's derivatives held a great deal of spiritual significance.

More recently Lyall Watson and Karel Drbal popularised the notion of "pyramid power." The duo, whose theories developed something of a cult following throughout the 1960's and '70's, promoted the use of miniature pyramids for the supposed purposes of magical healing, enhanced psychic powers and communion with alien beings. Devotees of Watson and Drbal's theories believed that pyramids possessed a whole host of other strange and miraculous properties: that within a pyramid structure old razor blades would spontaneously sharpen, natural decay was delayed and germination rates improved. They also believed that a wish, written on a piece of paper and worn inside a pyramid pendant, would come true.

Today there are countless meanings attributed to modern pyramid structures: tributes to mighty civilisations, the step-by-step climb to knowledge, or a sinister symbol of the Freemasons and the Illuminati (see Part 2: The Illuminati and Milton Keynes) – a theme perhaps hinted at in George Orwell's foreboding pyramid shaped headquarters of the *Ministry of Truth* in *1984*. Alternatively, of course, there are many who see pyramids as nothing more than practical shapes which are pleasing to the eye.

Milton Keynes is home to a significant number of prominent pyramids and pyramid-like structures. The biggest and most obvious pyramid in Milton Keynes can be found at *The Point* entertainment complex. The Point, which opened in 1985, is most famous for being home to the UK's first multiplex cinema. The Point is built in the form of a ziggurat, but it is enveloped within in an illuminated, red, pyramid-shaped exo-skeleton: thus it is both a ziggurat *and* a pyramid.

The Point

Near The Point, in the Theatre District of the city, are another three permanent pyramid structures, perhaps representing the pyramids of Giza.

There are even more pyramids sited around the rear of the Milton Keynes gallery

Three pyramids in the Theatre District

One of several pyramids near the gallery

If the observant pedestrian takes a stroll along Silbury Boulevard, leaving the city centre and heading towards Campbell Park, one can find still further examples. The below pyramid is particularly noteworthy because, like The Great Pyramid of Giza, the 'capstone' is absent. A similar pyramid is seen on the American Great Seal and on the US dollar bill. A pyramid that is missing it's capstone is often associated, at least in popular culture, with Illuminati symbolism (see Part 2: The Illuminati and Milton Keynes).

Pyramid on Silbury Boulevard. Note the absence of a 'capstone'

Bletchley Leisure Centre (© Living Archive) Picture by Lawrence East-bury

From the 1970's until it's demolition in 2010, a very large pyramid structure housed the swimming pool at Bletchley Leisure Centre.

A tall, thin 'pseudo pyramid' sits atop the Belvedere in Milton Keynes (see Part 1: Midsummer Sunrise), dominating the city.

Whatever weight one wishes to place upon the meaning, power or symbolism of the pyramid, the sheer number and size of those in Milton Keynes leaves enough dark resonance to intrigue the most sceptical of minds.

The Labyrinth

A *true labyrinth* is very different from the sort of maze one would find at a modern theme park. In a true labyrinth there are no dead-ends or false paths, and no walls obscuring ones view: a true labyrinth consists of a single winding pathway leading imperceptibly from the entrance to the centre. Such true labyrinths – which were traditionally carved into turf - can be traced back over three and a half thousand years. In medieval Britain and Europe, labyrinths were associated with female deities and fertility rituals: during Easter, and other religious feasts, men would compete in timed races to the centre of the labyrinth where the village women waited. The labyrinths were also adopted as a symbol of the Christian faith, denoting the one true, if tortuous, path to eternal salvation. Few British medieval turf labyrinths survive today.

In Willen Peace Park, one can find *The Willen Maze*, which was designed by landscape architect Neil Higson. The path in this turf maze, one of the largest true labyrinths in the world, is two miles long and takes over half an hour to complete. The maze has four lobes at the cardinal points of the compass, each of which contains a bronze face designed by sculpter Tim Minnett, and which is said to represent the four main races of mankind.

The patterns of many ancient turf labyrinths, as well as The Willen Maze, bear a striking similarity to the Buddhist and Hindu *mandala* – a circular pattern used in sacred art work to depict the spiritual realm and aid meditation.

At the centre of The Willen Maze grows a single oak tree. Few trees are more symbolic than the oak, which has long represented strength and courage. The Romans thought that oaks attracted lightning, hence they connected the oak to the sky god Jupiter and his wife Juno, the goddess of marriage – leading the oak to be further associated with conjugal fidelity and fulfilment: it is largely because of this association that pagan marriages were conducted under the boughs of the oak. Socrates considered the oak to be an oracle tree, and the druids ate acorns in preparation for prophesying. The druids also thought the oak tree had the power to heal and renew strength.

The Willen Maze is an enlarged replica of the ancient Saffron Walden Rosicrucian Maze.

The Rosicrucians were a secret society founded in medieval Germany. They held a philosophical doctrine built upon supposed lost esoteric truths of the ancients, which were said to provide an insight into all aspects of science and spirituality. Groups claiming Rosicrucian heritage and insight have existed for hundreds of years, and there are also those who claim a close contemporary Masonic or Illuminati association exists (see Part 2 The Illuminati and Milton Keynes).

Part of the Labyrinth with the oak sapling in the centre

PART 2

The Illuminati and Milton Keynes

A city aligned with the midsummer sun; a city which straddles an established ley line; a city which is home to a labyrinth designed by a medieval secret society; a city riddled with standing stones and occult pyramid structures (see Part 1). Is this plethora of idiosyncrasies simply coincidence? Or are these unusual features merely the tip of the iceberg – a tantalising glimpse of a deeper, hidden layer of planning.... of a *conspiracy*?

The many curiosities of Milton Keynes take on far more sinister connotations when considered in the context of the *Illuminati*. In addition to those facets already mentioned, conspiracy theorists the world over have identified countless purported links between the Illuminati and Milton Keynes.

There are so many conflicting facts and legends concerning the existence, presence and influence of the Illuminati, that it is hard to pin down a definitive explanation. According to mainstream historians, the Illuminati was a secret society established in Bavaria in the late seventeen hundreds. The movement advocated philosophies typical of the Enlightenment era from which it was born – free thought, secularism, liberalism and republicanism, and it recruited heavily from the very Masonic lodges which it sought to structurally emulate. The vision of the founder, university professor Adam Weishaupt, was for the organization to infiltrate the upper echelons of society and become an intellectual and political elite for the betterment of mankind. Despite a handful of notable members, however, the Illuminati was just one of many of secret societies in existence at the time. It wasn't long before these societies came to be seen as a fledgling threat to the Bavarian monarchy and the Roman Catholic state religion. Less than a decade after its inception, in a general crackdown on secret societies, the Illuminati was itself infiltrated and broken up by government agents.

Conspiracy theorists have a different take on the history of the organisation. They believe that the Illuminati not only survived the state repression, but went on to achieve the society's original aim – namely to exert a covert influence on world affairs through a powerful membership. It is this version of events which forms the basis for many modern conspiracy theories. Today, conspiracy theorists credit the Illuminati with everything from the orchestration of wars to financial collapse, revolution and the spread of AIDS. The Illuminati are believed to have engineered these events – and many others - not for the betterment of mankind, but to further alternative and more nefarious aims. These alternative aims can range from the financial self-interest of the membership, to the eventual creation of a 'One-World-Government' (under the so called *New World Order*). The most extreme conspiracy theorists even go so far as to argue that the Illuminati are in the employ of extraterrestrial or reptilian masters, and that they are preparing the way for eventual alien domination of the planet.

The alleged membership of the Illuminati can encompass anyone of significant international influence, from British nobility and American

Presidents, to international bankers and financers such as the Rocker-fellers and the Rothchilds.

There are myriad associated tales of Illuminati ritual, belief, practice and symbolism – much of which is associated with the occult. Some conspiracy theorists assert that the seventeenth century Illuminati group was simply an infamous temporary embodiment of an other-wise nameless – albeit timeless – cabal whose origins have been lost in the mists of pre-history. These theories hold that the druids are at the very least in cahoots with – if the not direct forbears of - the Illuminati – using their own esoteric knowledge, and that borrowed from other ancient mystery religions, to provide an unbroken line of spiritual guid-ance and ritual oversight stretching back to the dawn of civilization. Whatever the truth – or otherwise – of these theories, it is perhaps easy to see where the Milton Keynes connections can be made.

The Initials 'MK'

For some, the very initials *MK*, by which the city is commonly known, are, in themselves, sufficient to arouse suspicions.

In the 1950's the American CIA began a series of top secret mind control experiments on often unwitting American and Canadian citi-zens. The code name for this project was MK-ULTRA (uncannily simi-lar to the codename '*ULTRA*' which was applied to the high level, top secret intelligence produced by Bletchley Park, Milton Keynes, during the Second World War). The techniques used during MK-ULTRA in-cluded the surreptitious administration of drugs and other chemicals, hypnosis, sensory deprivation, isolation, verbal and sexual abuse, as well as various forms of torture. The project came to public attention in a 1975 Congressional enquiry. During this enquiry it was revealed that the director of the CIA had ordered all MK-ULTRA files to be de-stroyed two years earlier, in 1973, a fact which not only hampered the enquiry, but also fuelled the conspiracy theories.

It was later established that MK-ULTRA grew out of *Operation Pa-*

perclip, a secret project set up in 1945 to recruit former Nazi scientists, many of whom had studied mind control techniques, behaviour manipulation, torture and brainwashing. Whilst the full details of MK-ULTRA may never be known, it is thought that one aim was to create a so-called 'Manchurian Candidate' – an unwitting assassin who has been brain washed to commit political murders. Whilst the CIA officially insists that mind-control-type experiments have long been abandoned, there are whistle-blowers such as Victor Marchetti who claim this is not the case.

Other top secret operations with the MK prefix include:-

- MK-NAOMI – a joint US Department of Defense/CIA research programe into biological warfare which ran throughout the 1950s to the 1970s.
- MK-DELTA – the code name for the use of MK-ULTRA materials and techniques which were deployed on foreign (as opposed to US) soil.
- MK-SEARCH - a project dedicated to developing 'truth drugs' for use during interrogations.

In popular conspiracy lore, the MK-ULTRA mind control program was run by the CIA under the guidance of the Illuminati – who, of course, pull the strings of all such CIA operations. The Illuminati now use the mind control techniques perfected by MK-ULTRA (particularly those utilizing subliminal messages and triggers planted in the popular media) to control, enslave and program politicians, celebrities and ordinary people. The communal brainwashing of an entire model community, via subliminal messages, is a theme which was explored in the 2009 novel *Candor* by Pam Bachorz.

Strange that in 1967 a major new city, built upon an American grid system, should be known as 'MK' – the prefix of some of the most secretive CIA projects *which were then operational.*

MK – a veiled reference to *'Mind Kontrolle'* for those in the know, or simply coincidence?

The Rothschilds

The House of Rothschild is an enigmatic, long established, and exceedingly rich European family. Having established their mega fortune through banking and finance, the Rothschild dynasty - whose membership boasts many members of the British and Austrian nobility - is widely regarded as one of the most influential and wealthy cadres on the planet. Perhaps because of this extreme power and affluence, the Rothschilds have, for over two hundred years, been subjected to many accusations of Illuminati membership.

In 1967 the Milton Keynes Development Corporation (MKDC) was established in order to plan and develop the new city. In 1971 Evelyn Robert de Rothschild was appointed Deputy Chair of this non-democratic and largely unaccountable body. He held this post until 1984.

Coupled with the many unique features of Milton Keynes (see Part 1), the early appointment and long tenure of a Rothschild into a senior position on the MKDC has provided fertile ground for those wishing to link the city with the Illuminati.

The Russells

The Russell Family, holders of the *Duke of Bedford* title, are another ancient, extremely affluent and notable clan who have endured regular allegations concerning their Illuminati status.

As well as their noble titles and considerable establishment ties, the Russells have historically maintained extensive property portfolios in and around the locale - the most famous of which is the current family seat of Woburn Abbey.

Echoes of the Russell family influence can be found in street names throughout the city: in addition to a *Tavistock* Street (*The Marquess of*

Tavistock being the courtesy title of the Duke of Bedford's heir apparent), a *Duke* Drive and a *Woburn* Avenue, there are also a number of byways named after *Russell* and *Bedford*. To the conspiracy theorist this plethora of family references represents nothing less than the subtle marking of a territory.

Eyes Wide Shut

A recurring theme amongst conspiracy theorists is the link between Milton Keynes and the 1999 Tom Cruise / Nicole Kidman movie *Eyes Wide Shut*.

The movie Eyes Wide Shut is thought by some to be a veiled exposé of the Illuminati. In the movie, Tom Cruise plays a doctor called Bill Harford, who tricks his way into a masked orgy which is apparently being held by a secret society. At the party various sinister, cloaked and masked individuals participate in a series of seemingly pagan, semi-religious (or sacrilegious) rituals and indulge in multiple public sexual acts. Harford's cover is blown, and as he is expelled from the party he is warned that if he reveals or investigates what he has seen both he and his family will suffer dire consequences. Harford ignores the threat, and his subsequent enquiries result in mysterious deaths, disappearances and further cryptic warnings. He is finally dissuaded from further investigation by an insider who reveals that there are many important and powerful people who wish to keep their involvement in the secret society quiet.

The main conspiracy theories linking Eyes Wide Shut with the Illuminati broadly run as follows:-

- The movie is an allegory of the Illuminati: a secret, quasi-occult society, whose membership is drawn from a powerful elite.
- The obvious themes of deniable wrong-doing and occult ritual are based upon purported Illuminati practices.
- The movie title itself is an Illuminati 'code phrase'. Members

use this phrase amongst themselves as a reminder to curb their
- testimony against one another. This working principle allows
  the Illuminati to continue operating above the law.

There are few elements of Eyes Wide Shut which have not been subject to analysis and interpretation by dedicated conspiracy theorists. Under such close observation the movie has been completely disassembled and, from the minutiae, countless further observations have been made: that pentagram images can be seen in background scenes, that the names of characters are veiled references to Illuminati legend and lore, that the phrases, words and gestures used throughout the movie point towards Illuminati contrivance. The movie is seen as a two fingered salute to the Illuminati, a warning shot letting them know that they have been rumbled.

Eyes Wide Shut was directed by Stanley Kubrick who eerily died – some would say suspiciously – just four days after privately unveiling the movie's final cut. Conspiracy theorists have noted that not only did Kubrick's death occur exactly 666 days before the first day of the year in which his most famous film (*2001: A Space Odyssey*) is set, but also that various scenes in the movie appear to predict or mirror his demise.

The Illuminati / Eyes Wide Shut link to Milton Keynes is primarily based upon an unusual statue, ominously named *Dangerous Liaisons*, which sits in the Theatre District of the city. A prominent masked character who features in one of the ritual scenes in Eyes Wide Shut bares an exact likeness to this statue. There appears to be no logical reason for the presence of a such a sinister statue in the middle of the city, and no explanation is given on its plinth, leading some to surmise that the movie has picked up on yet another Illuminati pointer.

Warner Bros refused to allow an image of the movie character to appear in this book for comparison.

'Eyes Wide Shut' statue in the Theatre District

Owls

Owls have long been regarded as a powerful symbol of the Illuminati. Speculation abounds as to the history which sits behind this adopted 'logo', but one of the most common theories is that which draws upon the facts known about *Bohemian Grove*.

Bohemian Grove is a wooded Californian compound of nearly three thousand acres which belongs to the *Bohemian Club*.

The Bohemian Club, which was established nearly one hundred and fifty years ago, is an exclusive men's club whose alumni includes many former US Presidents, senior government officials, business leaders and other influential individuals and families. The Bohemian Club hosts regular 'summer camps' at Bohemian Grove where these powerful movers and shakers can put the pressures of their professional life behind them unwind away from prying eyes. It was at one of these camps that the foundations of the top secret Manhattan Project – the United

States' nuclear bomb programme – were laid. The summer camp, which has been infiltrated by journalists on a number of occasions, kicks off with a heavily stylized 'ceremony' in front of a forty foot tall concrete owl, during which the members 'cares' are ritually cremated. The owl – which is the mascot of the Bohemian Club – is said to represent wisdom. Some commentators have alleged that the Bohemian Club owl is actually a shrine to *Molech*, an Old Testament pagan god. Others, however, believe that the ritual is nothing more than a harmless, tongue-in-cheek custom during which the members can metaphorically cast off the constrictions of daily life; it is a precursor to a few days of hard drinking and student-like high jinks.   Nevertheless, given it's secretive nature, elite membership and unusual rites, the Bohemian Club is often perceived to be some kind of 'front' for the Illuminati.

Occult owl worship at Bohemian Grove aside, the owl clearly represents the Illuminati's predilection for operating quietly in the shadows, whilst also embodying the virtues of watchfulness, secrecy and power. Whatever the truth, the fact remains that as a powerful predator, sitting at the top of the food-chain, the owl seems the perfect symbol of choice for an organisation which maintains a silent overview of a largely ignorant prey.

To the Illuminati hunter, owl symbolism is not confined to a secretive grove in California, but can be seen everywhere – in architecture, on statues, on television and even on money. The Illuminati reveal their omniscience through their symbols – hidden in plain sight, but visible everywhere to those 'in the know'.

There are a number of owls overlooking Milton Keynes. The owl below is one of two which can be found looming over shoppers from it's roost in the skylight of the multi-story car park behind The Food Centre. There is an identical owl watching over Queens Court.

Cynics would argue that these Milton Keynes owls are simply present to deter pigeons: the conspiracy theorist, however, would point to their palpable lack of success in this endeavour (as evidenced by the number of pigeons present, and the fact that the owls themselves are covered in pigeon muck) and argue that this is just a convenient and plausibly deniable cover story.

One of at least three owls looking down upon the city centre

Obelisks

Obelisks feature throughout the ancient world, and have been venerated by all the great civilisations. They were particularly cherished by the Egyptians - to whom they represented both the sun god *Ra* (the obelisk being seen as a petrified ray of sun), as well as the phallus of *Osiris*, the Egyptian god of the afterlife, the underworld and the dead.

Even today, obelisks are often sited in key seats of power. Some of the most famous such structures include the Washington Monument in the capital of the United States, Cleopatra's Needles - which are split between London and New York, the Vatican Obelisk in Saint Peters Square, Rome, and the Luxor Obelisk in Place de la Concorde, Paris. Other obelisks, both old and new, can be found in virtually every major capital city in the world.

Obelisks are frequently associated with the Illuminati, particularly by those who emphasize their occult roots. The conspiracy theorist perceives an obelisk as a physical stamp of Illuminati presence, a highly visible flag which asserts domination of a strategic site.

A giant, Illuminati-style obelisk can be found right in the middle o

Great Holm, a Milton Keynes housing estate built in the 1980's. In the absence of a plaque to explain its purpose or meaning, the Great Holm Obelisk is often assumed to be yet another sign of Illuminati occupation.

Great Holm Obelisk in Milton Keynes

Najaf

The Iraqi holy city of Najaf is home to the tomb of *Imam Ali*, cousin and son-in-law of the prophet Muhammad. It was Ali's death which spawned the birth of the Shia Islamic sect. The city, which has been described as the 'Vatican of the Shia,' is one of the most hallowed sites in the Middle East, with only Medina and Mecca attracting more Muslim pilgrims every year. Najaf is home to the largest cemetery in the world: many devout Shia Muslims aspire to be buried there in the hope that they may be raised alongside Imam Ali on Judgement Day. Long before the birth of either Islam or Christianity, Najaf was a major centre for Sumerian and Babylonian mystery religions.

Given Najaf's religious, historical and socially strategic status, it should come as no surprise that the Illuminati are purported to have an interest in the city.

The Illuminati are often accused of engineering conflict in pursuit of their 'divide and rule' strategy. Such warmongering also supports Illuminati investments in the so called *military-industrial-complex*, allowing the network to profit financially from the spoils of war.

In 2004 Najaf was reduced to ruins during a three week assault by American troops.

In 2006 the planners responsible for designing Milton Keynes – a city which many were convinced was modelled according to Illuminati blueprints - were contracted to redesign Najaf.

To the conspiracy theorist this is evidence of classic Illuminati methodology in action: the war waged in Iraq, on the false premise that the country was harbouring weapons of mass destruction, ultimately opened the door to an Illuminati power-grab in one of the holiest and most unstable regions on Earth.

Onwards and Upwards

Aside from the widely accepted Illuminati infiltration of Masonic lodges in the 1700s, the links between the Illuminati and the Freemasons are the subject of much debate. Many conspiracy theorists hold that the Freemasons are little more than an administrative, or 'feeder' branch of the Illuminati.

In 1923, Manly Palmer Hall, a Canadian mystic and 33rd degree Freemason (the highest honour recognized under the Scottish Rite) published *The Lost Keys Of Freemasonry,* a book of instruction for the aspirant Freemason, and of reference for the uninitiated. One of the most controversial and oft quoted passages from this tome is as follows:-

*"When the Mason learns that the key to the warrior on the block is the proper application of the dynamo of living power, he has learned the mystery of his Craft. The seething energies of Lucifer are in his hands and before he may step **onward and upward**, he must prove his ability to properly apply energy."*

'The Lost Keys Of Freemasonry' by Manly P. Hall

The book cover features a picture called "The Master Mason" by J. A. Knapp. 'The Master Mason' depicts a robed figure with his arms raised in the air. Overlooking the Milton Keynes cricket pavilion, on the edge of Campbell Park, is a statue called 'Onwards And Upwards'. The statue resembles a native American totem pole, and on the top is a cloaked figure raising both arms in the air. The statue bears a striking similarity to the cover image from Manley Palmer Hall's book, and it is also remarkable for the fact that its name (Onwards And Upwards) appears o be lifted from Hall's most controversial passage.

Co-coincidence, or yet another subliminal Illuminati flag?

The Master Mason by J. A. Knapp
(Courtesy of Philosophical Research Society, Inc., Los Angeles, CA, www.prs.org)

Onwards And Upwards

Street Art

The dove - although seen in Christian tradition as symbol of peace - does in fact have a much older association, particularly in Illuminati lore, as a symbol of sacrifice. This stems from the use of doves as burnt offerings to God, as described in the Old Testament.

At the entrance to The Centre MK (the main city shopping mall) lies a depressed circle with markings indicating the cardinal points of the compass. Set above the circle are three mysterious engravings. Each engraving appears to show an anonymous, faceless individual offering up a dove to the sun.

Given the probable occult leanings of the Illuminati, their respect for ancient sun gods such as *Ra* (see Part 2: Obelisks), and their love of druidic ritual and secrecy, it doesn't take a great stretch of the imagination to conclude that an engraving of a faceless, anonymous figure 'offering up' a dove to the sun is - in fact - Illuminati imagery symbolizing sun worship.

One of three engravings featuring faceless figures

PART 3

Cryptozoology and Alien Invaders

In its purest sense cryptozoology is the term applied to *the study of hidden animals.* This includes animals in the following categories:-

1. Those which are generally considered to be extinct - such as the woolly mammoth.
2. Mythical animals - such as the Loch Ness Monster.
3. Animals living wild in geographical locations which are far removed from their natural habitat - such as alligators in the New York sewers.

All such animals are referred to as 'cryptids'.

An *alien invader* is a non-native species which settles and thrives in an unnatural environment – often to the detriment of native species (for example the grey squirrel was introduced from North America and now outcompetes our native red squirrel).

The dividing line between alien invader and the third category of cryptid can be a fine one. A small number of cryptids will naturally be difficult to spot, and their existence may be disputed. As their numbers increase and their existence becomes widely accepted, they may later be re-classified as an alien invader.

Over the years, many cryptids and alien invaders have been reported in Milton Keynes and its environs.

Wallabies

Whilst wallabies, the diminutive cousin of the kangaroo, are native to Australia and New Guinea, small feral mobs can also be found through-out the British Isles.

One of the most famous British breeding populations can be found in the Peak District. The Peak District wallabies are descended from a small group which escaped from a wildlife park during the second world war. Likewise, there are over one hundred feral wallabies cur-rently living in the Ballaugh Curraghs area of the Isle of Man, all of which are descendants of a single pair of escapees which fled a wildlife park over forty years ago.

Elsewhere, these antipodean marsupials have been purposely intro-duced. Lady Colquhoun released a wallaby family onto Inchconnachan Island, in Loch Lomond, Scotland, in the 1940's, and in the 1980's Dub-lin Zoo exiled a small herd of excess stock to Lambay Island in the Irish Sea. Both populations are self-sustaining to this day.

Small, but successful, troops of wallaby are also known to exist in the Teignmouth area of Devon, Ashdown Forest in Sussex, and on the islands of Bute and Lundy. The origin and size of these groups remains unclear, and the genial nature of the wallaby, combined with their lack of ecological impact, means that no national census nor formal record of their spread exists.

Wild wallabies have been reported in and around north Milton Keynes for a number of years. A white wallaby has been seen, photographed and even caught on video in the vicinity of Olney on several occasions. A family of wallabies has been spotted near the M1 Newport Pagnell Services, and reliable sightings of individuals have also been documented in Stoke Goldington.

Albino wallaby in Olney

Red Deer

Red deer are the largest native British mammal. They are usually found in the Highlands of Scotland and other remote rural areas. In 2008, however, a rampaging twenty stone, six foot tall stag made national headlines when it brought rush hour traffic to a halt in the urban centre of Milton Keynes.

Concerned about the threat to both the stag and to motorists, police and wildlife experts closed off city roads as they tried to catch the beast. At one point marksmen had the stag in their sights, but were unable to fire tranquilizers for fear of endangering the public. Despite it's enormous size, the stag managed to evade it's hunters by running down underpasses and leaping fences. It is assumed that it later made its way back out of Milton Keynes via the city's extensive green corridors.

Stag loose in the centre of Milton Keynes
© Geoffrey Robinson/Rex Features

Alien Big Cats

Mysterious big cats have been spotted prowling the UK for at least four decades. Due to their clearly non-native status they have been termed *Alien Big Cats* (or ABC's) by cryptozoologists. The most famous of the many British ABC's are perhaps the Beasts of Bodmin and Exmoor, and the Surrey Puma.

The commonest explanation for the presence of ABC's is that many big cats were released into the wild following the introduction of the

Dangerous Wild Animals Act in 1976. The Act imposed strict conditions on the sale and possession of big cats, making the ownership of the beasts prohibitively expensive for many. There are numerous types of cat believed to be roaming the wilds of Britain today, the biggest of which may be panthers, pumas and lynx. If one accepts the reality of their existence, it is a matter of some speculation as to whether these cats are the descendants of those liberated in the 1970's, or whether they owe their freedom to more recent, unreported releases and escapes from un-licenced collections. Either way, sightings of ABC's are reported on a regular basis - and dozens of photographs and video clips exist which purport to show the beasts in the British countryside.

Hard evidence for the presence of British ABC's surfaces from time to time:-

- In 1975 a clouded leopard was caught alive in Kent.
- In 1980 a puma was captured alive in Inverness-shire, Scotland.
- In 1988 a leopard cat was shot in Devon, and a swamp cat was killed crossing a road in Hampshire.
- The following year (1989) a jungle cat was found dead on a road in Shropshire.
- In 1991 a Eurasian lynx was shot dead in Norfolk after killing fifteen sheep.
- In 2001 a Eurasian lynx was caught in the suburbs of North London.

The *Milton Keynes Beast*, which is consistently described as large black cat, was first reported in Bleak Hall in 1986. The sightings picked up over the following ten years, and 1996 still stands out as the single most significant year for big cat encounters in the city. One of the first sightings of that summer was made by a local dog walker – Roger Calderwood BEM - who's story is as follows:-

"We were due to go to the Alps that morning so that I could climb

Mont Blanc, so I took our German Shepherds out for a walk at about 5.30-6.00am prior to taking them to the kennels. I went down the canal and up around Campbell Park. I walked up from the canal bridge along the top path towards CMK (Central Milton Keynes) and just after the cattle grid I turned right onto a bridle path which leads down the hill, around a copse and then reaches the bottom path nearest the ornamental gardens and Silbury Boulevard.

'It was a beautiful, bright, sunny morning and very peaceful. I turned right onto the bottom path back towards the Pavilion. To my left was a four foot high metal rail fence (which is still there) with a swing gate into the gardens – it's too tall for dogs to jump willingly. As I walked along, the copse was now to my right. I was always very cautious about meeting other dogs and kept a good watch in case my dogs got boisterous. Suddenly I saw a black creature come out of the copse, across the open grass towards the fence and gardens. It was about fifty metres away and I had a clear view from slightly uphill. Initially my reaction was 'oops another dog' so I grabbed hold of my two dogs. I then watched what I can only describe as a black puma, with a very long tail, walking low to the ground. It moved swiftly across the open ground to the fence - which it jumped over in one effortless stride - and disappeared into the gardens. I was shaking and I couldn't believe my eyes! I put the dogs on leads and ran home. When we came back from the Alps two weeks later, the 'Citizen' (local Milton Keynes newspaper) was on the doorstep with front page headlines of several credible big cat sightings (e.g. driving instructor - pupil and passenger - when it crossed the road in front of their car). I phoned the (police) control room to report my sighting and they laughed at me. But I know what I saw! It was a Puma."

The story does not end there, however, because in addition to being a resident of Milton Keynes, Roger was also a full time police officer in the city – and this was not to be the last of his dealings with the beast.

"(Later that year) I was on 'nights' on what was then known as the South Sector of the city. A call came in at about 0530am from two security guards who were working on the building plot for what must have

been Tesco's at Kingston. They reported that they had just seen a big cat. The police dog handlers were deployed, and because of my previous experience I volunteered to attend too.

'The two security guards were white as a sheet, and were so scared they had locked themselves in a shed! Both I and the other officers present were convinced of their integrity. They (the security guards) told me it had crossed a freshly cut grass area and crossed a car park before jumping over a mound of earth diggings and disappearing into the building site. Sure enough, across the start of the car park there were four clumps of wet grass cuttings spread out at equal distances. They had pad prints still clearly visible in the grass which had fallen off it's pads onto the hard surface. I then looked at the earth mound which was in fact a big pile of clay about four inches high, and on the other side I found a print. It looked like a big cat print to me. Because it was in moist clay I got a spade and dug it out."

As one of Thames Valley Police's trained Wildlife Officers (a responsibility held alongside his regular police role), Roger continued to investigate the sighting. He took the footprint to the Scenes of Crime Office, who made an inverted cast from it. A couple of days later Roger took the dinner-plate-sized cast to nearby Whipsnade Zoo, where he had arranged to meet the big cat expert. Together they examined the cast and compared it with many other prints.

"I was told that these animals have a hunting area of about sixty square miles. This would easily cover Milton Keynes and Cambridgeshire, where there had also been many sightings at that time. The conclusion, given the provenance of the story, was that my print cast was definitely a puma or black leopard paw print. It was definitely not a manmade hoax."

Sightings have continued sporadically ever since. In 2006 a large, black, leopard-like creature was reported in Howe Park Wood in Tattenhoe, and in 2010 a big cat was seen in Springfields. Given the long history of the purported sightings, it is possible that the city falls within the territory of more than one big cat.

Escaped Marmosets

In 2009 a marmoset hit the national headlines when it was discovered watching television in a living room in Bedford Road, Aspley Guise.

The monkey, which was swiftly re-captured, was one of a pair who had escaped from nearby Woburn Safari Park. The second escapee was never found. Marmosets – which are normally around six inches tall - are native to the rain forests of south east Brazil.

Escaped Marmoset from Woburn Safari Park

Guinea Pigs

Guinea pigs, as all children know, are popular pets throughout the UK. They originate from the South American Andes - where they have been domesticated and bred for food for thousands of years.

In the early 1990's it was widely rumoured that a new-born male and female guinea pig had been dumped upon Northfield Roundabout near the Milton Keynes Coachway. Stranded on the traffic island, this pioneering pair is said to have produced a whole herd of feral, albeit inbred, offspring.

Whether this tale is fact or urban legend remains unclear, and given the crepuscular nature of the shy cavies, it is difficult to verify their current status on the island. It is probable that any guinea pigs which might have existed either perished, or moved on, during the large scale local road works of the late 1990's. But then again it is not implausible to suppose that they sat tight.

It is certainly possible that a colony of guinea pigs *could* flourish on the roundabout. Northfield Roundabout is plenty big enough to support a large population of feral rodents; there is ample natural tree cover - and more than enough grass and dandelion on which to graze. Guinea pigs are timid explorers and the high, steep concrete sides of the roundabout would deter all but the bravest from making any attempt to flee. Any resident guinea pigs would also be relatively safe from predators: the roundabout's status as the busiest in the city – crawling with M1 traffic all day and night - would make most foxes (and crytozoologists!) think twice about setting foot there. Female guinea pigs are fertile from about four weeks old, and breed readily all year round, so it is not hard to imagine a thriving population existing on this physically isolated plot!

Northfield Roundabout today: somewhat tidier than in the early 1990's

Poisonous Spiders

Over one hundred years ago, false widow spiders arrived in the south west of England on banana shipments from the Canary Islands. The false widow, which is now Britain's most poisonous spider, found the British climate conducive and has been slowly spreading east ever since.

Closely related to the deadly black widow spider, for which it is often mistaken, a bite from the false widow can cause chest pain, nausea and vomiting which frequently necessitates hospitalization.

In 2011 Milton Keynes trading standards pest control unit confirmed that the spiders had finally crawled as far as Milton Keynes. The announcement followed the discovery (and destruction) of a nest of false widow spiders in a domestic Bletchley residence.

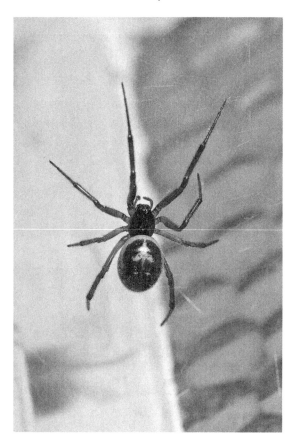

A false widow spider
© Marc Baldwin (Wildlife Online)

Ring Necked Parakeets

Ring necked parakeets are medium sized green parrots, native to the foothills of the Indian Himalayas. The ring necked parakeet is Britain's only naturalized parrot, and in the south east of England there are breeding flocks numbering in the hundreds: it is estimated that there are over fifty thousand wild parakeets in London alone. They seem particularly drawn to suburban areas, where they readily take advantage of garden bird feeders.

Given the increasing numbers of parakeets around the capital and the southern Home Counties, it is perhaps inevitable that they should now be spreading north through cities such as Milton Keynes.

Over the past few years regular sightings of pioneering ring necked parakeets have been made in and around Tattenhoe, Furzton Lake, Howe Park Woods, Caldecotte Lake and Stony Stratford. Given their success elsewhere, it is likely that their presence will only increase.

Ring necked parakeet in Tattenhoe

Terrapins

Red eared terrapins are native to North America. In the late 1980's and early 1990's the popularity of the *Teenage Mutant Ninja Turtle* comics, books and movies lead to a surge in the popularity of red eared terrapins as children's pets. When interest waned, thousands of these terrapins – which can grow to over a foot long – were released into the wild: many survived and can still be found living feral across the UK today.

There have been many sightings of terrapins on the Grand Union Canal, particularly in Wolverton, where they can be seen basking in the sun during the height of summer. Sightings have also been recorded in Willen Lake. It is thought that the climate in the UK is too cold to allow them to successfully breed but, with a life expectancy of around thirty years, red eared terrapins are sure to be a feature of local water ways for many years to come.

A pair of red eared terrapins in Wolverton

American Signal Crayfish

As it's name suggests, the American signal crayfish is native to North America. In the 1960's and 1970's several crayfish farms sprung up in the UK to supply the restaurant trade. Numerous individuals either escaped or were released, and they began to colonize water ways throughout the country, particularly in the south. Today, these highly aggressive, armour-plated invaders can be found throughout much of southern Britain. So prevalent are these crayfish in Milton Keynes, that every autumn the Parks Trust and the Environment Agency host a popular 'Crayfish Day' on the banks of the River Ouse in Stony Stratford. Competitions are held to see who can catch the most mini-lobsters (the biggest of which can exceed seven inches in length), and many unfortunate captives are served up in al fresco cooking displays. At the close of the day the Environment Agency take the excess catch away for 'disposal'.

The American signal crayfish is bad news for the environment. They devastate native fish stocks by devouring young fish, fish eggs and even the weed on which the ill-fated eggs are laid. They also carry a 'crayfish plague' to which they are immune, but which has wiped out much of Britain's diminutive native *white claw crayfish.*

An American signal crayfish, caught in Stony Stratford weir

Alien Fish

Native to central and eastern Europe, the carnivorous *wels catfish* can – under ideal conditions - grow ten feet long and weigh over three hundred pounds. There are ancient legends which claim that people have been eaten by these giant fish. Whilst the veracity of such stories is questionable, there are substantiated reports of swans, ducks and even small dogs being swallowed as they swim innocently across the surface of catfish infested waters.

Illegal to release into the UK, there are nevertheless many confirmed reports of these monsters being caught in the Grand Union Canal, Willen Lake and Bradwell Lake. The biggest catfish in Milton Keynes, some of which tip the scales at over seventy pounds, have been captured by specialist anglers in Great Linford Lakes.

Wels catfish are particularly fond of eating the American signal crayfish (see Part 3: American Signal Crayfish), a fact which raises the intriguing prospect of an alien species hunting another alien species within the Milton Keynes water ways.

A wels catfish caught by Brian Smalley

Brown goldfish /carp hybrid – note the elongated tail

Smaller, and infinitely prettier, than the giant wels catfish is the common goldfish. An innocuous first pet for millions of children - but when released into the wild goldfish can become an invasive pest, causing havoc with the natural ecosystem. Feral goldfish, which generally lack or lose their familiar orange colouration, are known as 'brown goldfish', and can reach two feet in length. They breed readily with common and crucian carp, producing fertile hybrids. Like the wels catfish, brown goldfish can be found throughout ponds and lakes in Milton Keynes, and are especially prevalent in Wolverton Mill.

Strange Jelly

For hundreds of years a strange, jelly-like substance - which is said to evaporate or disappear shortly after it has fallen - has been reported throughout the UK and other parts of the world. Historically known as *the rot of the stars* or *star jelly* due to the belief that it had fallen from meteor showers, this mysterious goo is particularly prevalent in and around Newport Pagnell.

Theories abound as to the true origin of this gelatinous slime: some have postulated that birds have eaten frogs and toads, and then regurgitated the toxin filled oviducts. Others suggest that the substance is a type of mould, animal vomit, afterbirth, or even an alien or paranormal agent. Tests on the matter have proved inconclusive, and whilst the jelly is generally accepted to be of organic origin – the only indisputable fact is that nobody knows for sure where it comes from.

'Star Jelly' in a field in Newport Pagnell

PART 4
Strange Religion

Paganism, witchcraft, relics and miracles: many would associate these arcane faces of religion with forgotten corners of an enchanted, medieval England. In the shadowy backwaters of modern Milton Keynes, however, one will find that such curious phenomena are still very much alive and kicking.

Witches, Pagans and Satanists

The word 'pagan' derives from the Latin word 'paganus' which literally means 'country dweller'. As Christianity spread throughout the known world, the last vestiges of the 'old', often earth-based, religions were gradually confined to isolated rural pockets. Hence *pagan* developed into a catchall phrase used to describe all who did not worship the Abrahamic Christian God, and in particular those who practiced indigenous religions. There are now so many variations of the old cultures, beliefs and sects – that it is impossible to point to any single defining rite, characteristic or ideology as unequivocally *pagan.*

Sitting under the pagan umbrella is the witchcraft religion known as *Wicca.* Wicca, as a religion, rose to prominence in the 1950's and 1960's, although its adherents generally claim cultural lineage to pre-Christian European witch-cults. Whilst there are many different Wiccan denominations or 'traditions', they generally share a number of common beliefs and practices. Wiccans are frequently organised into *covens* which are headed by a high priest and priestess. Most Wiccans believe in the existence of magic, which they aspire to influence through witchcraft rituals and spells.

From the fifteen hundreds to the seventeen hundreds, thousands of people were tried and executed for witchcraft though-out Europe. The power of the witches curse was widely feared. Today we can see parallels between the popular perception of 'old' dark European witchcraft and the modern practices of *juju, muti* and *kindoki* – witchcraft beliefs prevalent throughout sub-Saharan Africa which often lead to murder and cruelty. The association with black magic, Satanism, the casting of hex's and other wicked practice is, however, one which most contemporary Wiccan witches reject, preferring instead to align themselves more closely to the New Age movement than the traditional evil arts.

Perhaps it should come as no surprise to learn that Milton Keynes, a city built upon heathen principles (see Part 1) is a hotbed of paganism and witchcraft of such of pre-eminence as to make Matthew Hopkins, the notorious seventeenth century Witchfinder General, turn in his grave.

In 1994 Milton Keynes hit the national headlines when the city council became the first in the country to give formal permission for a Wiccan coven to worship on public land. Martin Prop - witch and high priest of a coven simply known as *The Milton Keynes Wiccan Coven* - submitted an application to allow his coven to worship openly on waste ground near the back of Elfield Park. After much debate, and in the face of fierce protest by Christian groups, as well as a petition signed by over three thousand objectors, the council narrowly agreed to approve the plan. The application submitted by the coven outlined details of the planned rituals, giving a unique insight into modern Wicca practice.

The application revealed that in the darkness of the early hours each member of the coven would dress in robes: candles would be placed at the four corners of the site, and a small open fire would be lit (this would provide light, burn incense and warm up food such as jacket potatoes). The robes worn by the coven were left to personal preference, although those worn by the high priest were white. The high priest would carry a *besom* (traditional witches broomstick) and a ceremonial dagger – the latter being used to 'channel the life forces in blessings of people or things'.

The council's permission was granted on the condition that no more that twelve ceremonies were held each year, and that the coven limited the number of participants to a maximum of twenty.

Having now been turned into a nature reserve managed by the Parks Trust, the land is no longer used for these formal Wiccan ceremonies.

The Medicine Wheel Stone Circle on the shore of Willen Lake (see Part 1: Standing Stones and Neolithic Monuments) has been a regular focal point for city witches for many years. Large, well organised sabbats (ceremonial gatherings of witches) are held at the site to mark Wiccan festivals, the most significant of which is the summer solstice. From midsummers eve into midsummers day, dozens of robed witches – both independent practitioners as well as those from established covens – come together at the stone circle to welcome the rising sun. Wiccan priests and priestesses, complete with ceremonial daggers, staves and broomsticks, preside over the festivities and perform various dark rites in the firelight.

Less formal moots or *esbats* (as the smaller gatherings are known) also occur at the stone circle on the first night of every full moon. Pagans and witches attend these casual 'moon moots' to engage in largely uncoordinated, music, prayer, earth-based worship and meditation.

City witches celebrating the summer solstice at the Medicine Wheel (© Tony Margiocchi)

Various other city pagans have formed a loose alliance known as the *Bubbling Pot* project. The Bubbling Pot's aim is to raise money to buy woodland in which to build another stone circle. Such a privately owned altar would allow pagans to conduct more radical ceremonies, free from any restrictions that might be imposed by landowners such as the council or the Parks Trust elsewhere in the city.

Milton Keynes' single most famous independent witch passed away in 2011. Dorothy Griffiths (or *Madam Morgana*, as she liked to be known) served - alongside her husband Reg (also known as *Merlin of Avalon*) - as a councillor on Stantonbury Parish Council for many years. The pagan couple lived in a house known as the *Dragons Lair*, and in between organizing psychic fairs, clairvoyance sessions and parish council meetings, the White Witch of Buckinghamshire practiced benevolent magic in a bid to heal the world. When Reg died, in 2007, he was laid in state, in full ceremonial robes, for two weeks, before Dorothy officiated at his pagan funeral in front of four hundred mourners.

In 2012 Stantonbury Parish Council announced plans for the construction of a memorial garden dedicated to Dorothy's memory.

Such is the level of witchery in Milton Keynes, that there is even a shop specialising in witchcraft/Wiccan supplies. On St Johns Street in Newport Pagnell, one can find an outlet known as 'Wyrdos' where the city's witches go when they need a new hazel wand or other such paraphernalia.

In addition to it's covens and independent witches, Milton Keynes is also home to a number of pagan biker gangs, the best known of which is *Cernunnos*. Cernunnos, meaning *horned one*, takes it's name from a horned Celtic god, who is also known as the 'Stag Lord' or 'Lord of the Hunt'. A light was shone upon the Milton Keynes pagan bikers when Peter 'Big Pete' Wilkins died in 2011. Big Pete was a well-known pagan druid who was heavily associated with the local biker community. Hundreds of bikers attended his pagan funeral service at the city's Crown Hill crematorium.

There are some in the city whose practices and beliefs sit far beyond 'simple' paganism and witchcraft: on the extreme dark edge of the religious spectrum are the *Satanists*. In 2005 hundreds of Satanists descended on Milton Keynes in support of a Satanic music night held at *The Pitz* nightclub. Headlined by American black metal band *'Deicide'*, the event - which was well represented by the Milton Keynes branch of the *Church of Satan* - drew protest and criticism from Christian groups across the region. Given the highly controversial nature of their 'Church', the city's Satanists – like those elsewhere - maintain a very low profile even today.

Relics

Some of the world's most ancient and holiest relics can be found in Milton Keynes.

A 'holy' relic is generally understood to be a body part of, or an object associated with, a saint or other holy person. The faithful believe that relics possess not just a spiritual energy, but often the powe r of healing or other miracles. Many Christian churches used to house relics, and at one point they were promoted as a major draw to pilgrims – who provided a significant source of income. Elaborate 'reliquaries' were constructed to house these holy curiosities. The cult of relics largely came to an end in Britain during the Reformation.

Christianity has never stood alone in the veneration of relics, with all major religions having their own holy objects. Buddhism is no exception. After Lord Buddha's death, over two and a half thousand years ago, his body was divided into portions and enshrined in *stupas* – large buildings built specifically as reliquaries. Many of these relics, believed to be the original remains of Buddha's body, can still be found in *stupas* today.

The Peace Pagoda, which sits in the Milton Keynes Peace Park on the shore of Willen Lake, is one such *stupa*.

Built in 1980, by the monks and nuns from the nearby Nipponzan Myohoji Buddist Temple, the Peace Pagoda was the first of its kind to be built in the Western Hemisphere. The ornate building enshrines sacred relics of the Buddha, which were presented from Buddhist communities in Nepal, Sri Lanka and Berlin.

Surrounding the Pagoda, and adding to the overall holiness of the place, are a thousand cherry trees and cedars, which were donated by a town in Japan, as well as saplings propagated from the sacred Bohdi tree, under which the Buddha attained enlightenment.

Few places in Europe can claim such an ancient and holy Eastern bounty.

The Peace Pagoda, which enshrines the relics of Buddha

Glastonbury Thorn

Milton Keynes is home to one of the holiest and most miraculous trees of British Christian lore – the 'holy' *Glastonbury thorn.*

The original Glastonbury thorn grew exclusively in and around Glastonbury, Somerset: it is identical to a normal a hawthorn in all but one respect - the Glastonbury thorn blossoms twice a year. The first miraculous blossoming occurs at Christmas to mark the birth of Christ, and the second blossoming occurs at Easter to mark the resurrection.

Legend holds that Joseph of Arimathea visited Glastonbury after the ascension of Jesus. He is said to have thrust his walking staff into the ground at Wearyall Hill, whereupon it miraculously sprouted: thus the Glastonbury thorn was born. Every Glastonbury thorn which is alive today is a propagated descendent of this very tree. Some versions of the legend assert that the staff was made from the cross on which Christ was crucified, and others that it was a stick owned by Christ Himself.

Today, the three best known holy thorn trees of Glastonbury can be found in Glastonbury Abbey, on Wearyall Hill, and in the grounds of the Church of St John – the latter being Glastonbury's current 'official' holy thorn tree, a flowering sprig from which is sent to the Monarch every Christmas.

The 'original' Glastonbury thorn, at Wearyall Hill, was cut down and burned by Cromwell's puritan troops during the English Civil War as part of their campaign against relics and old church superstition (see Part 4: Relics). Glastonbury's other iconic holy thorn trees have also befallen natural deaths and vandalism over the years: fortunately, however, these trees have invariably been replaced by stock propagated from the original lineage. Interestingly, Glastonbury thorn seeds and cuttings do not generally share the parent tree's gift of a miraculous second blossom, instead reverting to the flowering pattern of a 'normal' hawthorn. The only way to propagate the tree, and retain the miraculous characteristic, is through grafting – the blackthorn tree being the favoured rootstock.

Milton Keynes is unusual in being one of the very few historical homes of the miraculous thorn tree outside of Glastonbury itself. In the aptly named 'Holy Thorn Park', which sits on 'Holy Thorn Lane' in Shenley, next to the children's playground, one can find Milton Keynes's very own Glastonbury thorn tree. The tree was originally planted here due to the proximity of St Mary's Church, an ancient Grade Two listed church which has existed - in some form or other - since at least 1223 AD. The presence of the Milton Keynes holy thorn tree has coloured local folklore for many years, and has inspired the name of the local 'Glastonbury Thorn School'.

The Glastonbury thorn in it's 'enclosure' in Milton Keynes

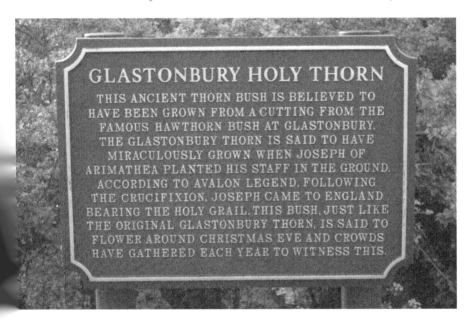

GLASTONBURY HOLY THORN

THIS ANCIENT THORN BUSH IS BELIEVED TO
HAVE BEEN GROWN FROM A CUTTING FROM THE
FAMOUS HAWTHORN BUSH AT GLASTONBURY.
THE GLASTONBURY THORN IS SAID TO HAVE
MIRACULOUSLY GROWN WHEN JOSEPH OF
ARIMATHEA PLANTED HIS STAFF IN THE GROUND.
ACCORDING TO AVALON LEGEND, FOLLOWING
THE CRUCIFIXION, JOSEPH CAME TO ENGLAND
BEARING THE HOLY GRAIL. THIS BUSH, JUST LIKE
THE ORIGINAL GLASTONBURY THORN, IS SAID TO
FLOWER AROUND CHRISTMAS EVE AND CROWDS
HAVE GATHERED EACH YEAR TO WITNESS THIS.

*Sign by the Milton Keynes holy thorn detailing the legend of it's
origins*

Deanshanger Holy Spring

The village of Deanshanger, which sits to the west of Milton Keynes, is famous for it's holy springs, the first of which is supposed to have been miraculously created by Saint Thomas Becket.

In 1162 AD Thomas Becket became the twenty seventh Archbishop of Canterbury. Shortly after his appointment a power struggle began to develop between the Church and King Henry II. Becket fought any attempt to weaken the Church's links with Rome and to make it more accountable to the Crown. As a result, the Archbishop fell out of favour with the King and, in October 1164, Henry summoned Becket to appear before a great council at Northampton Castle to answer charges of contempt of royal authority and malfeasance in the Chancellor's office. Becket was convicted, but fled the castle and escaped to the continent.

Between escaping from Northampton Castle and crossing the channel, Thomas Becket - disguised as a peasant - sought refuge in the Gilbertine Monastery in what was then the hamlet of Deanshanger. As the Archbishop approached Deanshanger, he was recognized by a farm labourer who saw through his disguise. Knowing of Becket's purported ability to perform miracles, the labourer complained to Becket that the water supply in Deanshanger was foul and stagnant, and he pleaded with the Archbishop to intervene - just as he had supposedly done in nearby Northampton. Taken with the man's plight – and in no position to argue - Becket looked to Heaven, and struck the ground with his staff: at that very spot a clean water spring appeared instantly. The creation of this miraculous spring in Deanshanger is one of the seven hundred and three miracles attributed to Becket that lead to his canonization.

PART 5

Hauntings and the supernatural

Given the number of ancient buildings and settlements incorporated into Milton Keynes, it is perhaps inevitable that ghosts and hauntings should abound. The rapid and on-going expansion of the city means the Reaper is becoming an ever-more frequent visitor, and as the toll of human souls grows, so surely does the city's already heady capacity for supernatural lore.

Haunted Building in Fenny Stratford

During it's heyday, the landlord of the Old Bull pub in Fenny Stratford would often open up the cellar to find that barrels and other items had been moved around during the night. In an attempt to get to the bottom of the mystery, he sprinkled powder across the floor, but the mysterious movements continued – albeit no footprints were ever found. The Bull later became the 'Entertainer', which closed in 2009. The building has since been reopened as a craft shop.

Since the building's change of use, strange occurrences have continued, with the current staff reporting on-going unexplained phenomena. Despite having no toast making or cooking facilities, the overpowering aroma of fresh toast can sometimes be smelled in localised spots throughout the building. Leading into the eaves of the ancient building is an ill-fitting door which is notoriously difficult to open: so stiff is the door that it frequently has to be prised open with a screwdriver, yet on a number of occasions it has been inexplicably opened overnight. Even when the shop is occupied the door has been known to fly violently open of its own accord - the bang being audible throughout the building. The manager of the wool department, on the top floor, has reported that specific balls of wool – left out overnight - have mysteriously disappeared come morning. In spite of these spooky carryings on, the staff don't consider the presence to be malicious. When the staff have planned new displays, or changed fixtures and fittings, they have

The former Old Bull in Fenny Stratford

found that existing furniture seems to have already been moved - ever so slightly – as if to accommodate the planned change: they have light-heartedly attributed such small events to the benign, if somewhat mischievous, spirit. The only time the ghost has unnerved anybody in recent times was after a member of staff - who 'definitely' left the lavatory seat down before locking up for the evening - found that it was raised up when she opened the shop the next day!

The Phantom Trolley Lady

Although now demolished and replaced by housing, there was once an RAF Camp in west Bletchley. Within the camp was a Sick Quarters, and throughout the 1950's many patients reported hearing the sound of a trolley being wheeled through the ward during the night. Some witnesses even observed the phantom trolley being pushed by a ghostly woman in a green uniform: the apparition apparently travelled the length of the ward before disappearing through a door.

Olney Castle

The old Castle Pub at the north end of the Olney High Street is now an Indian Restaurant. In the late 1900's the pub and it's environs were haunted by the ghostly form of a black-clad woman. A ghostly man was also seen to walk through a locked door. An exorcism was performed, but a few years later the ghostly woman was seen again.

The Devil in Olney

Just north of Olney, one can find *Whirly Pit*- a purportedly bottomless pond. From time to time – at the hour of midnight - a phantom coach, pulled by four headless horses and driven by a decapitated coachman, is believed to pass through Olney (possibly through the old Castle Pub – see Part 5: Olney Castle). The Devil is said to be the only passenger in the

The Old Castle Pub in Olney

Former residence of Lucifer, Olney High Street

coach. When the coach reaches Whirly Pit it plunges into the water and continues it's journey underground by means of a secret passage which leads to Goosey Bridge. At Goosey Bridge the diabolical coach emerges violently into the open, churning up the meadow as it breaks free. There are those who claim that if one stands in the meadow the swaying and shuddering can be felt at any time of the night or day.

The Devil was, it seems, so taken with Olney that he would frequently assume human form and visit the town – even going so far as to take up residence there. He is said to have lodged in a large house on Olney High Street (where numbers 121, 123 and 125 now stand). An old woman, who lived in the house opposite, could see into Lucifer's rooms if she leaned out of her attic window, and from this vantage point she would frequently spy on his activities. On one occasion, upon noticing the woman's nosy antics, the Devil used his evil power to cause an enormous pair of horns to sprout from the old woman's head. The horns were so big that she was unable to pull her head back inside the window until the Devil deigned to remove them. The Devil's privacy was soundly observed after this incident.

Whilst living on Olney High Street, Lucifer was said to be a regular drinker in the street's 'Two Brewers' Pub. He would bully and humiliate the landlord, and his presence understandably caused would-be-patrons to steer well clear of the establishment. It was, apparently, not an easy task for the landlord to 'bar' the Devil from his pub, and so thirteen priests - equipped with bells, bibles and candles - attempted to negotiate a settlement on his behalf. The priests met with the Devil and suggested a one hundred year 'ban' from the pub. The Devil considered this somewhat excessive, and refused. One priest therefore asked the Devil if he would consider a shorter, voluntary, ban. He asked the Devil if he would…

"….postpone your visits until this candle I hold in my hand is burnt out?"

The Prince of Darkness replied in the affirmative, whereupon the wily priest immediately blew out the candle and threw it into a well. The Devil has not been seen in the pub since.

The Devil's former favourite 'local'

Dick Turpin

The Old Swan Inn at Woughton On The Green is believed to have been a regular safe house for legendary highwayman Dick Turpin. The pub's prime attraction, so far as the infamous thief was concerned, was it's proximity to *Watling Street* (the current A5) - a main route from London to Chester – which provided a plentiful supply of wealthy merchants upon which to prey.

Dick Turpin's ghost now haunts the roads and ancient paths in the vicinity of the pub. Sightings of the restless spirit vary, with some witnesses reporting him pacing the road on foot, whilst others put him astride a horse. Most report the apparition as resembling a dark figure wearing a trademark tri-corn hat, but one in particular describes him as wearing a fancy waistcoat, cloak and riding boots. Beside the Inn is a large stone, which it is said Turpin would stand upon to mount his horse. The stone is purportedly cursed, with a dreadful fate awaiting anyone who tries to move it. It is reported that one (un-named) person who tried to move the stone was involved in a terrible road accident a week later.

Local legend holds that on one occasion Dick Turpin waited at the Swan Inn whilst a local blacksmith reversed his horses shoes. Turpin subsequently pulled off a daring robbery and the reverse tracks left by his horse led *to* the scene rather than *away* from it. This confused Turpin's pursuers, allowing him to escape.

The Old Swan Inn is also said to be haunted in it's own right. During redecoration, decorators placed all the chairs on the table tops over-night, only to find they had been mysteriously returned to their original positions by morning. A one-time-owner reported being regularly awoken at night by the sounds of talking and laughing from downstairs: when he descended the stairs, the noise of the party would cease. The owner's wife also observed an apparent 'customer' walk through a wall. Numerous drinkers have, over the years, reported being shoved or pushed by invisible assailants.

Ye Olde Swan at Woughton on the Green - literal haunt of Dick Turpin

Dick Turpin's 'mounting stone' - the indent of a footprint still visible

The Old Swan Inn sits directly opposite 'Turpyn Court'

The ghost of Dick Turpin is also associated with a house called *Wood field* on Weathercock Lane in Aspley Guise. Over two hundred year: ago an Inn or house is believed to have stood upon the site. The dwell ing was occupied by a father and daughter. When the father went out, the girl would invite her lover around. One day the father came home unexpectedly and, in a futile attempt to avoid being caught together, the lovers hid in a cupboard. Knowing full well where the lovers were hiding, the father pushed heavy furniture against the door, trapping them until they died of thirst.

The legend holds that some years later Dick Turpin broke into the house when he was looking for somewhere to hide, whereupon he discovered the bodies. Turpin subsequently used the knowledge of his discovery to blackmail the father into providing him with both periodic refuge as well as money - which he supposedly re-distributed to the poor. The house is not only haunted by the ghost of Dick Turpin and the beating hooves of his horse, but also by the cries of the dying lovers. It has been suggested that at some point the bodies of the lovers were removed from the cupboard and buried beneath the floor of the cellar. During World War Two a fifteen year old girl called Doreen Price – who was staying at the house as an evacuee – claimed she had seen the spirit of the dead girl reaching out to her in the cellar.

These ghostly tales first came to light in the late 1940's when the owner of Woodfield, a gentleman by the name of Blayney Key, appealed against the rates he was paying on the house, which had been set according to it's value in the late 1920's. Key argued that he could not let the house because it was so haunted. The case for re-valuation went to a hearing where a maid gave evidence that she had seen ghostly arms coming out of the wall whilst she tried to sleep. Despite this claim, the case was thrown out. Whether these ghostly legends are true or were simply invented in an attempt to reduce the property rates is a subject which has, over the years, prompted heated debate as well as many séances and ghost hunts – the results of which have proved equally controversial

Ghosts of Newport Pagnell

The Kings Arms pub sits on Severn Drive in Newport Pagnell, near the site of a long demolished twelfth century priory. Some years ago the landlord of the pub asked a local photographer to take a picture of the new menu board which hung above the bar. When developed, the photograph appeared to show a hitherto unseen monk standing at the end of the bar. The same landlord frequently sensed a mysterious presence in the periphery of his vision, and on one occasion saw a shadowy apparition moving along the hallway. More often, however, the 'presence' would disappear whenever he turned to look directly at it.

Subsequent landlords have experienced further spooky phenomena, such as the strange behaviour of their dogs which would stare, transfixed, at a pool table near the bar as if watching some unseen visitor. From time to time witnesses positioned outside The Kings Arms have reported seeing dark figures moving in upstairs rooms: upon later examination the rooms have been found to be empty.

Cemetery Bridge, the footbridge leading from the Newport Pagnell's *Church of St Peter and St Paul* to the sprawling *New Cemetery* is said to be haunted by the ghost of a woman. She can sometimes be seen standing on the bridge, watching people as they pass underneath on Ousebank Street. Over the years hundreds of coffins must have been carried across this bridge en route from church funeral to their final resting place, and to this day one can observe the 'coffin-shelves' under the bridge arches, where undertakers would discretely rest their charge in the event of a previous funeral overrunning.

Next door to the Church of St Peter and St Paul is the old *Odell's* restaurant. The building, which has now been renamed and rebranded as a Thai eatery, has long been held to be haunted by the benevolent ghost of an elderly lady called Emily - who it is said died in a fire many, many years ago. The ghost of Emily tugs at the clothing of unsuspecting customers and staff.

The Kings Arms, Newport Pagnell

Part of Cemetery Bridge, Newport Pagnell

Odell's restaurant as it is today

At the bottom of Newport Pagnell High Street sits the Police Station Generations of officers serving at the police station have reported eerie and unexplained noises echoing around the building, and to this day many report sensing a 'presence' about the place, particularly in the old cell block. The station was built in 1872, and in the early days the Superintendent or Inspector would live there with his family. Evelyn Louis Dibben was one such resident Superintendent. After a long and painful battle with bowel cancer, the unfortunate police officer died in the police station on the 9th February 1922. Throughout his illness, the dedicated officer refused to abandon his post and go on the sick-list. Some speculate that the ghost of the late Superintendent Dibben remains as dedicated to the station today as he did during his lifetime.

Superintendent Dibben

On the 15th January 1960, newly promoted Newport Pagnell Sergeant, George Bickerton, attended a multiple, albeit minor, road traffic accident on the southbound carriageway of the M1 motorway, four miles north of the police station. As Sergeant Bickerton and his colleagues cleared the stricken vehicles from the road, a passing car skidded and ploughed into the men. Forty year old Sergeant Bickerton was rushed to Northampton General Hospital where he sadly died of his injuries. Sometimes, late at night, a car can still be heard to drive into the back yard of Newport Pagnell Police Station: the back door of the building then opens, and footsteps ascend the stairs. Upon inspection, no one is to be found upon the stairs, and no cars are present in the rear yard. Station legend holds that this is George returning to book himself off duty.

Sergeant George Bickerton

Newport Pagnell Police Station

Passenham

The haunted hamlet of Passenham sits just across the river from Stony Stratford.

The Manor of Passenham was acquired by Sir Robert 'Bobby' Bannister in the early sixteen hundreds. Bannister immediately saw his newly acquired tenant farmers as a licentious bunch, a failing which he blamed on three centuries of ineffective supervision from non-resident landlords. Determined to put an end to his subject's independent ways, Sir Robert quickly developed a reputation as a cruel and intolerant master. One of Bannister's first acts was to raze the village to the ground, leaving just *St Guthlac's Church* and a couple of farmhouses intact: the destruction was intended to exempt his properties from the Poor Rates. His next act was to enclose the surrounding fields. Bannister's unpopularity was not helped by the fact that he was a keen royalist in what was an otherwise parliamentarian stronghold.

One night, whilst out hunting, the unpopular Master fell from his horse and broke his neck. With his foot caught in the stirrups, his steed dragged him to the churchyard. As Bannister lay dying, the priest offered him the opportunity to confess his sins and receive absolution. Sir Robert held out for too long, and passed away un-shriven.

Later, as the Sexton was digging his grave, the ghost of Bannister appeared beside him wailing: *"I'm not yet ready."* Despite this irregularity, the burial went ahead, and as the coffin was lowered into the grave the small group of mourners heard the same eerie phrase ringing out.

Following his burial, the phosphorescent spectre of the broken-necked Bannister was to be seen nightly, dragged in the stirrups of a ghostly horse which disappeared amongst the gravestones of St Guthlac's Church. So persistent and so terrifying was this nightly visitation, that the Bishop and a number of other clerics were called to perform an exorcism. Tales vary as to the success of this deliverance, with some claiming that the ghost was banished altogether, whilst others that the visitations simply became more infrequent.

St Guthlac's Church, which has stood for over a thousand years, and is considered to be one of the most important archaeological churches in the country, is haunted by numerous other ghosts besides that of Sir Robert Bannister. The organ has been known to play of it's own accord, the bell rings out at random, and several apparitions have been seen in the vestry.

Passenham Mill, which sits just a stone's throw from St Guthlac's Church, is supposed to be haunted by the restless spirit of Nancy Webb. Nancy Webb, who lived in nearby Deanshanger (see Part 4 Deanshanger Holy Spring), lost her husband in the Crimean War in the late 1850's. Shortly after the death of her husband, Nancy tragically lost her infant son. Both husband and son were buried in the church yard of St. Guthlac's. Overcome with grief, Nancy visited the graves continually. Eventually the poor girl went mad and, on the night of the Deanshanger Village Feast, whilst the locals were enjoying the festivities, Nancy threw herself into Passenham Mill. The wheel dragged Nancy under the water and crushed her to death. Local legend has it that at midnight on the night of the Deanshanger Feast (which is still held every October) screams can be heard emanating from the Mill.

The haunted St. Guthlac's Church, Passenham

Passenham Mill

Fairies

In times gone by, the existence of fairies was accepted as fact. They weren't the diminutive, winged, Disney-esque sprites that we think of today, but were instead malicious, supernatural entities which were able to assume many different forms.

People lived in fear that fairies would steal unbaptized human babies to raise as their own, or that they would abduct human women for wives. The wicked fay would leave *changelings* in the place of their victims – senile and twisted fairy folk who took the form of the stolen family member. Adults and infants thought to be changelings were regularly killed by their own families. As recently as 1894 a woman in Clonmel, Ireland, was burned to death by her husband in the belief that she was such a changeling. People developed many rituals and customs to keep the fairies at bay – cold iron, oatmeal and rowan were believed to deter the sprites, and wearing one's clothes inside out confused them by somehow hiding the identity of the would-be-victim.

Bow Brickhill Woods, which is now part of Milton Keynes, was once a reputed fairy stronghold. One tale of the impish little folk asserts that Bow Brickhill's *All Saints Church* was originally intended to be built upon the Village Green. Every night, during the church's construction, the fairies would move all the bricks to the top of a huge nearby hill. Eventually the builders gave in, and built the church upon the brow of the hill, exactly where the fairies had left the bricks. It is not known exactly when the church was built, but it is thought to have existed since at least the twelfth century.

Today, the sounds and sights of civilization are eliminated by the ancient woodland which envelops the brow. In the overgrown graveyard, it is easy for visitors to imagine that time has stood still. Such is the seclusion and natural beauty, that if anywhere in the modern world can still claim to host fairies, then the churchyard and the enchanted woods in which it sits are surely prime contenders.

All Saints Church in the fairy woods at Bow Brickhill

Situated north east of Newport Pagnell, adjacent to both the M1 motorway and the River Great Ouse, and just south east of Mill Farm, lie some comparatively recently excavated Bronze Age barrows. Local legends say that fairies can be summoned by walking around these barrows nine times.

Bradwell Windmill

Bradwell Mill is situated on Nightingale Crescent in the Bradwell district of Milton Keynes, and has a somewhat curious supernatural association.

In 1685 the daughter of a local miller was courted by two young men. One of her would-be-suitors killed the other in a fit of jealousy, and he was subsequently gibbeted for the murder. Shortly afterwards the young girl herself was found dead in her father's mill. Her ghost is now said to haunt Bradwell Mill.

Interestingly it would have been impossible for the girl to have died in the current building, because Bradwell Mill was not built until 1817 when local entrepreneur Samuel Holman decided to capitalize on trading opportunities opened up by the recent completion of the Grand Union Canal. It is not known whether there was some sort of mill on the site previously, or whether the girl lived in another mill altogether (prior to the construction of the windmill it is probable that water mills were used, relying on the River Ouse or Bradwell Brook). Equally, it is not clear what - or who - the restless spirit of the unfortunate miller's daughter haunted for over a century before the new windmill was built!

Bradwell Windmill

PART 6

The Unexplained And The Bizarre

From ancient curses and unexplained disappearances, to macabre deaths and literary intrigue, there is a long and constantly evolving history of *weirdness* which has – over the years - befallen, perplexed or shocked the good people of Milton Keynes.

Cursed Elm Tree

The ancient village from which the city of Milton Keynes takes it's name has now been swallowed up by the administrative district of *Middleton*. At the centre of Milton Keynes Village is The Green, and upon The Green – adjacent to the Swan Inn – there once stood a four hundred year old elm tree.

Village tradition held that the tree was cursed: if the tree should die, no further babies (some versions specify boys) would be born within the village boundaries.

In the late 1980's the magnificent tree fell prey to Dutch Elm Disease and began to wither. By 1989 the unfortunate elm – now barely clinging to life - was hit by a car involved in a high speed police pursuit. The combination of disease and car crash finally spelled the end for this once fine specimen.

Records of village births since tree's demise are extremely sketchy, with any that might have occurred being formally attributed to the greater 'Middleton' district of the city. The nearby Milton Keynes General Hospital opened it's doors in 1985, making it statistically likely that the vast majority – if not all - births to mothers from Milton Keynes Village would – by 1989 - be occurring at the hospital's maternity unit rather than in the old village itself. None of the midwives currently working in the city can recall ever having been present at a home birth in Milton Keynes Village.

Whatever the truth behind the curse, it is a strange turn of fate that the demise of the tree should go hand in hand with the opening of a modern maternity wing outside the ancient village boundaries.

A Sad Epitaph

The church of St Mary Magdalene in Stony Stratford burnt down in 1742. The shadowy, overgrown graveyard and the crumbling church tower still remain however – providing a quiet and eerie retreat in an otherwise bustling little town. A corpse was buried in the graveyard beneath a stone bearing the following epitaph:-

Here lies a body who did no good,
And if it had lived it never would,
Where it has gone and how it fares
Nobody knows and nobody cares

The identity of the body below this ancient stone remains a mystery, as does the story behind the grim testimonial.

The dilapidated remains of St. Mary Magdalene's church tower

Disappearing Goats

Willen Lake is one of the largest purposely built 'balancing lakes' within the UK. Along with a number of smaller lakes, it was constructed to protect Milton Keynes from flash floods along the river Ouzel. Within the lake are some very deep 'ponds' to protect the fish population during periods of drought. Willen Lake is formed of two parts, the southern lake and the northern lake – which are connected by a thin causeway. The southern lake is managed as a leisure facility, with sailing and wakeboarding being popular. The northern lake, however, is designated as a nature reserve and is home to a very large undisturbed island – Willen Lake Island - which is notable for a number of peculiarities.

The city ley line (see Part 1: Ley Lines) appears to end (or begin) on this island, and public access is banned. Boating and swimming are prohibited in the north lake and, even if one were so inclined, access to the island by boat would be extremely problematic due to the wide and reed infested shallows which blanket the edge of the lake.

The island is a nationally renowned nesting habitat for migratory water-foul. To maintain this appeal, it is necessary to manage the extensive scrub which – if left unattended – would quickly overwhelm the island. Due to the difficulties associated with regularly accessing this isolated haven, a herd of goats was marooned upon the island in 2004 as a form of natural bramble control.

The goats thrived until a mysterious incident in 2007 when – overnight – half of them simply 'disappeared'. An investigative mission to the island was undertaken by officials from The Parks Trust – who found the remainder of the herd in a very distressed state. The officials ruled out an accident, and no bodies were ever found. They also ruled out escape, pointing out that the goats had never previously attempted to swim the 90 meters to the shore, and that they were unlikely to voluntarily leave their herd. The fate of the goats remains a mystery to this day.

Willen Lake Island seen in the distance

The Blind Pond, Milton Keynes's very own Bermuda Triangle

The Blind Pond

In the Bow Brickhill area of Milton Keynes is a large pond-cum-lake known as *Blind Pond*. Blind Pond can be found just off the Woburn Sands Road, adjacent to the Blind Pond Industrial Estate.

According to legend, the pond has a history of inexplicably swallowing up unfortunate travellers. The best known victim of the Blind Pond dates back to the late nineteenth century when, one evening, a wealthy lady - together with her coach and four horses - mysteriously disappeared into the depths as they passed by. The whole party was swallowed in an instant, leaving not a trace. There are those who believe that the ghosts of this unfortunate travelling party now haunt the lake.

Strange Deaths

In 1997 Armando Merola was cleaning an eight foot deep mincing machine at the Beni Foods factory in Tongwell, Milton Keynes, when he slipped and fell in. A quick witted co-worker immediately switched off the power, but the gigantic machine spontaneously restarted, killing and mincing fifty-one year old Merola instantly.

In 2006 fifty-six year old engineer Hugh Drow was, ironically enough, conducting his daily safety check on a miniature railway at Milton Keynes's *Gulliver's Land*. After fixing a faulty door, Drow - who was on board the train at the time - stood up and gave the train driver a 'thumbs up' indicating that it was safe to proceed. The train therefore accelerated into a low roofed tunnel, decapitating the unfortunate Drow in the process.

In August 2007 a scene reminiscent of a horror movie was played out in the normally tranquil setting of the Willen Peace Park. Fifty year old Seiji 'Gyosei' Handa, chief monk at the Milton Keynes Nippon zan Miohoji Buddhist temple, was mowing the grass near the Peace Pagoda (see Part 4: Relics). For some unknown reason – perhaps to tinker with the grass cutting equipment - the monk alighted from the tractor-mower, and it drove off without him. Handa immediately set off in pursuit but, as he tried to remount the machine, he slipped under the blades and was chopped into pieces. The mower proceeded to drive the entire length of Handa's body, dragging him down the slope and leaving a trail of muscle, bone and other human remains scattered in it's wake. A crane later had to be used to lift the grass cutter from what was left of the monk. Bizarrely, this was not the first grass-cutting-related-mishap to befall the holy man: ten years earlier Handa had lost three of his fingers in a similar lawnmower accident.

Masquerade

In Midsummer Place, Central Milton Keynes, one can find a large clock which was designed by a gentleman called Kit Williams. The center-piece of this four tonne marvel, which incorporates a fantastical series of moving wheels and mechanical oddities, is an enormous frog. Every half hour - to the backdrop of a magical tune, the dropping of shiny balls and other automated curiosities - the frog comes to life and spurts forth hundreds of bubbles. Crowds of children eagerly gather to witness this spectacle. Quirky as the clock may be in it's own right, it also stands to remind the world of an international mystery which became an obsession for many during the 1970's and '80s.

In 1979, long before he designed the Midsummer Place clock, Kit Williams wrote, illustrated and published a book called *Masquerade*. The book, which became a worldwide bestseller, took the form of a children's fantasy puzzle: hidden within the rich illustrations were clues pointing to the whereabouts of a real life treasure which had been buried in a secret location in the United Kingdom. The plot of Masquerade revolved around the Moon (depicted as a woman) who falls in love with the Sun (depicted by a man). The Moon sends Jack Hare to deliver an amulet to the Sun as a token of her love. Jack Hare drops the amulet – a small gold and bejeweled hare - and the reader must unravel the clues to find it's real-world location.

Three years after the publication of Masquerade, the hare was 'found', buried in Ampthill, Bedfordshire, by a man calling himself *Ken Thomas*. Many of the passionate fans, who had bought into the cult of Masquerade, refused to believe that the hare had been found and convinced themselves that their own theories as to the location were correct: they viewed the 'find' as a mere feint.

Unknown to Kit Williams, Thomas – as it transpired in 1988 - was in actual fact one *Dugal Thompson*. Thompson was the business partner of *John Guard*, who was in a relationship with *Veronica Robertson*. Robertson had been the live-in girlfriend of Kit Williams when he had devised Masquerade. Thompson had discovered the location of the hare (which was sold at auction in 1988 for £31,000) not by following the clues, but by using inside information supplied by Robertson.

Despite the deception and controversy surrounding the amulet, Masquerade nevertheless inspired a whole host of subsequent armchair treasure hunts. Kit Williams remains an iconic figure to those interested in secrets, clues and mysteries, and the Milton Keynes clock stands as a permanent tribute to the work and imagination of this mystery-maker-extraordinaire.

Clock designed by Kit Williams

CONCLUSION

If the all the folklore, legends and tales are to be taken at face value, then one may conclude that Milton Keynes is the brainchild of a timeless, esoteric order. This dark network, whose existence is revealed through myriad hidden symbols, united a disparate group of haunted dells, and crafted them into a vast, occult-inspired playground.

In the quiet corners of this fantastical new city lives a veritable menagerie of exotic alien creatures. The mysteries of the ancients are exposed through obscure monuments which litter the estates, and witches and pagans indulge in long forgotten rituals in the shadows of the gleaming modern office blocks.

Modern Milton Keynes encompasses the holy, the unholy, the cursed, the unfortunate and the bizarre....

But then again, perhaps these idiosyncrasies are nothing but stories and coincidence, all molded together by fevered and mischievous imaginations to create intrigue and excitement in an otherwise vapid twenty first century void.

The truth, having long been lost in the mists of time and the confusion of the re-telling, probably lies somewhere between these two extremes.

Ultimately, only you can decide what to believe.

A city of secrets

What do these figures, forever sat outside Milton Keynes library, know that you don't?

ACKNOWLEDGEMENTS

The extent to which so many people, including complete strangers, were prepared to give up their time to assist me with researching and writing this book has left me feeling very humble and I am grateful to them all. A special thanks is due to the following people: Harry (a.k.a ukstormchaser / The Bug Whisperer) for the parakeet photo, Tom Langton for the terrapin photo, Roger Calderwood BEM who kindly took the time to relay his memories of the Milton Keynes Beast, Marc Baldwin (Wildlife Online) for supplying the photograph of the false widow spider, Lucy Kemp for the wonderful picture of a brown goldfish, Brian Smalley (from the Leighton Buzzard Angling Club) for allowing me to use a picture of his catfish, staff at 'Threads and Patches' who entertained me with their accounts of the benign spirit, Tony Margiocchi and Lawrence Eastbury for their pictures, Michael Shaw for detail concerning Newport Pagnell Police Station, the Philosophical Research Society and the Living Archive (in particular Herbert Booth) for their respective permissions, and of course my wife Sally for patiently enduring my incessant quest for wonderment. Last but by no means least my gratitude also extends to the unsung army who, perhaps understandably given the subject matter of this book, have requested that their contributions remain anonymous (they know who they are).

Printed in Great Britain
by Amazon